MW01628934

Bon Dance in Hawai'i

Dance with the Wind and the Spirits

First Printing, July 2004

Design by Sachi Goodwin

ISBN 1-56647-681-x
Library of Congress Catalog Card
Number: 2004107681

Mutual Publishing, LLC
1215 Center Street, Suite 210
Honolulu, Hawai'i 96816
Telephone: (808) 732-1709
Fax: (808) 734-4094
e-mail: mutual@mutualpublishing.com
www.mutualpublishing.com

Printed in Korea

This story was inspired by many.

To the "people of old":
Michael T. Suzuki, Naka & Yuji Miyamoto, Rose Suzuki,
Thomas Fujimura, Masao & Y. Miyamoto, Merle Howe, and Mildred Haworth:
Please keep dancing (and slamming the doors).

To my husband, and best friend, Mark:
Besame, besame mucho.

To my children: Jessica, Tucker, Max, and Tanner-Boy:
You are my inspiration; keep striving for big, colorful, and loud dreams.

To my nieces: Sophia, Maya, and Emma;
To my mom, Betty, Gail & Scott, Orrin and Jan:
What would I do without you guys? Kisses and hugs.

To my dear aunties: Faith, Eunice, and Nancy:
Thank you for your love and guidance.

To Ian & Judy and Law Offices of Ian Mattoch:
Thank you for the friendship and support.

To Jane Hopkins/Mutual Publishing, LLC:
Thank you for your endless patience, calmness, and direction.

To Anthony Lee:
Thank you for teaching me to not be afraid of color.

The people of old say that before Mānoa Valley had houses and families, before the valley had schools and stores, roads and cars, there were two types of wind: the wind of the land and the wind of the storm. But the valley has a third wind. No one can remember when this wind started to visit the valley once a year on sticky summer nights. This is a story of the third wind—the wind that dances with the people of the valley.

A silent breeze spilled over the mountain's edge, stirring the tops of trees, splashing through waterfalls and rushing through bamboo leaves making the trunks clack together. "Whoosh," whispered the wind. The bamboo trees bowed their greeting to the wind.

"Whoo...whoo...w...w...wake up," whispered the wind to a sleeping gecko. The gecko gripped a banana leaf as the wind flapped its waxy perch while rushing by.

In the valley, under a tree with red flowers, stood a house. The wind slipped through the house and slammed all of the doors closed. Tanner woke up with a start! It was Saturday! No work for his mom and dad. No school for Tanner and his brothers.

Tanner ran into his parents' room yelling, "What are we doing today? What are we doing today?"

"Get your brothers. We're going to a Bon Dance," answered Tanner's mother.

The wind wheezed out of the valley as it rushed toward the sea.

In between baseball games and piano lessons, Tanner and his family began the annual hunt for happi coats that didn't fit

and one-sided taikoboshi sticks. Calls to the aunties were made. Tanner couldn't wait for the Bon Dance!

Everyone met at the top of the road leading down to the temple. Tanner and his family followed colorful paper lanterns which led the way.

Once they reached the temple, they danced in a special circle around the yagura with a huge taiko drum that was bigger and louder than Tanner's dad! Tanner and his family followed women and men dressed in brightly colored kimono and happi coats. They stomped, twirled, and swung their arms to the rhythm of the taiko drum in a dance that told stories of a simpler time in a language that was strange to their ears.

In the still, summer night, a cool breeze flooded the valley. The banners and lanterns began to flutter and flap as the wind danced with Tanner and his family.

As they stomped and giggled while swinging small towels, the cousins told Tanner, "This is the dance that Grandma taught my mom and your mom when they were little girls. This is the dance that Great Grandma Rose and Great Grandma Naka danced to as children, when their families worked long, long ago on the plantations of Maui and the Big Island."

"Great Grandma Rose told us that every summer our ancestors who have died all come home. She said that we dance to welcome the spirits, to honor the spirits, and then we send the spirits safely back to another world." The wind sneaked up on Tanner and his family and gently blew their small towels in circles overhead.

Tanner and his family sat for a while and watched other people dance while they ate special foods: yakisoba noodles, andagi doughnuts, mochi,

and shave ice. Tanner's heart beat in the rhythm of the taiko drum, to the stomping of many feet, and to the clack of the taikoboshi sticks.

The circle moved together in waves of arms and smiling faces. Tanner and his family joined in the dance with the wind and the spirits of the people of old.

With full tummies and warm cheeks, Tanner and his family made their way back up the long, winding road that was lit by colorful paper lanterns. The evening mist cooled their backs as they walked to the beat of a distant taiko drum thumping deep in their hearts.

The wind and the spirits wrapped around Tanner's family as they walked back to their cars. Then the wind and the spirits blew over treetops, through the hills and roads of the valley, through the house under the tree with red flowers, and rushed out of the valley and headed toward the sea.

Together, the wind and the spirits drew in a breath and blew the sun over the horizon. In a rush to return to another world, silent, honored, and content, the spirits safely slipped away in a flash of green light.

The wind that danced with the people and the spirits of the people of old would have to wait another year until the taiko drum called them back to the valley.

Andagi Doughnuts

Okinawan Doughnuts

1 cup	Sugar
1 cup	Bisquick®
3 cups	Flour
1 tsp.	Baking soda
2	Eggs
Pinch	Salt
1 cup	Milk
	Oil (for frying)

Mix all ingredients together. Drop by spoonfuls forming round balls into hot oil. Coat with sugar, if desired.

Baked Coconut Mochi

1/2 cup	Butter, softened
2 cups	Sugar
1 tsp.	Vanilla
4	Eggs
2 cups	Milk
1 can (13.5 oz)	Coconut milk
3-3/4 cups	Mochiko flour
2 tsp.	Baking powder
1 pinch	Salt
1 sprinkling	Sesame Seeds

Cream together butter, sugar, and vanilla. Add eggs one at a time and beat until fluffy. Add milk and coconut milk to mixture. Add mochiko flour, baking powder, and salt. Mix together well. Grease 9" X 13" pan. Pour in mixture. Sprinkle sesame seeds on top. Bake at 350°F for approx. 1 hour.

Cut mochi with a plastic knife.

Yakisoba

Fried Noodles

2 cloves	Garlic
1 tbs.	Peanut oil
1 cup	Sliced ham or Portuguese sausage
5	Dried mushrooms, soaked and sliced
1	Round onion, sliced
1 pkg. (12 oz.)	Cooked noodles
1 pkg.	Bean sprouts
5 stalks	Green onion, cut into 1" lengths

Seasoning:

1 tbs.	Sugar
1/2 tsp.	Salt
1/4 tsp.	Pepper
2 tbs.	Soy sauce

Garnishes:

1 bunch	Cilantro (Chinese parsley)
1/4 lb.	Char siu (Chinese roast pork)
1	Egg, beaten, fried and sliced

Fry garlic in peanut oil. Remove when browned. Add ham, mushrooms, and onions. Add seasoning and fry together. Add noodles and fry until noodles are mixed well. Add bean sprouts and green onions. Stir until cooked. Remove to platter and garnish with chopped cilantro, char siu, and fried egg.

GLOSSARY

Bon Dance: A summer Buddhist festival that dates back 2,500 years in India. The history of the bon dance is attributed to the legend of a disciple of Buddha who, through the attainment of great insight, saw his deceased mother who had been reborn among the Hungry Ghosts of Hell. Due to the disciple's extraordinary practice of compassion and charity, he was able to save his mother from her fate. When his mother reached the shores of Nirvana, she danced with joy. The disciple and the other monks were so happy that they joined in the celebration with music, dance, and food in thanks for the reunion of the dead with the living.

In the Edo period (1603–1868) in Japan, the bon dance was performed around the typhoon season to represent the people's prayer for protection from typhoons, or "kaze-no-bon."

In Hawai'i, bon dances are a summer festival. Many of the songs and dances reflect the experiences of early Japanese immigrants in Hawai'i, and are celebrated by people of all nationalities, religious backgrounds, and ages. From late June until the end of August, a dance is held every weekend at a different temple.

Happi coat: A short jacket worn by workmen in Japan, it usually bears the employer's crest on the back.

Kaze-no-bon: "Kaze" means wind. "Bon" is the Buddhist All Souls' Day commemorating the dead.

Kimono: The kimono is the traditional clothing of Japan worn by men, women, and children. The cut, color, fabric, and decorations of a kimono vary depending on age, sex, and marital status. Style is also determined by the season of the year and the occasion for which the kimono is worn.

Mānoa: A valley in Honolulu, Hawai'i known for its mystical, rain forest atmosphere. There are many legends and stories of Mānoa Valley's people of old. Today, Mānoa is a tight-knit residential community that prides itself on its lush landscape, prestigious schools, and diverse religious, cultural, and economic population.

Taiko drum: Taiko drumming is the rhythm, movement, and spirit of the Japanese culture. It is said that in the olden days, Japanese village boundaries were set by the distance you could hear the taiko drum from the village temple. Taiko drumming was used in peasant festivals to mimic the sounds of animals, the wind, and the ocean in attempts to please or appease the spirits.

Taikoboshi: Two wooden sticks with red tape to be used in some of the bon dances featuring the taiko drum.

Yagura: The musician's tower used in bon dances.

ABOUT THE AUTHOR/ILLUSTRATOR

Jill Suzuki Haworth was born in Honolulu, Hawai'i. Her mother plays the piano, does yoga, tap dances, and has taught her that she could do anything if she sets her mind to it. Her father was an architect who taught her to draw and to always dream big. Her older sister, who is an architect and mother of three daughters, has always been her model for creativity and style. Jill has been married for twenty-two years to a man she fell in love with when she was sixteen years old while doing a high school production of Thornton Wilder's *Our Town.* They still hold hands when they walk on the streets of Downtown Honolulu. They have four children and live in a house in the back of Mānoa Valley under a huge tree with red flowers. *Bon Dance in Hawai'i* was written for her children and her nieces so they would never forget last year's Bon Dance when they danced with their grandfather one last time.

ARTIST'S NOTES

For this book, I used watercolor paints and Mānoa rain on Arches hot press, 140lb, natural white watercolor paper. Characters were outlined with Sharpie and Pigma Micron Permanent Pens.